DIAR[...] ROBLOX PRO

Ari
Avatar

SURVIVE THE ISLAND

SCHOLASTIC

First published by Scholastic Australia Pty Limited in 2023.
This edition published by Scholastic in the UK, 2024
1 London Bridge, London, SE1 9BG
Scholastic Ireland, 89E Lagan Road, Dublin Industrial Estate, Glasnevin, Dublin, D11 HP5F

SCHOLASTIC and associated logos are trademarks,
and/or registered trademarks of Scholastic Inc.

Published by Scholastic Australia in 2023.
Text copyright © Scholastic Australia, 2023.
Illustrations copyright © Scholastic Australia, 2023.
Cover design by Hannah Janzen.
Internal design by Paul Hallam.

ISBN 978 0702 33503 7

Printed and bound in Great Britain by Clays Ltd, Elcograf S.p.A
Paper made from wood grown in sustainable forests and other controlled sources.

1 3 5 7 9 10 8 6 4 2

www.scholastic.co.uk

MONDAY MORNING

SLUUUUUURP!

"Ugh! Coda!" I said groggily, wiping the dog drool off my face. "It's the

SCHOOL HOLIDAYS!

You don't need to wake me up, you know!"

I opened one sleepy eye and saw my dog looking down at me with bright, shiny eyes and a smile on her face. I couldn't be mad at her for more than ten seconds when she looked that **CUTE.**

I rolled my eyes and sat up, pulling her into a hug. She nudged me with her nose.

"I'm guessing nobody has fed you breakfast?" I said.

At the word 'breakfast', Coda's ears pricked up and she began to pant **EXCITEDLY.**

"OK, OK," I said, throwing back my blankets and stepping out onto the cold timber floor.

I walked down the stairs to the quiet **KITCHEN** below. Dad had already gone out for the day, taking a day trip to a reef to study some new marine plant life. He's a marine biologist, so that's part of his job. Mum was already in her gardening tools and was busy outside repotting her citrus trees. She loves spending time in her garden, and she'll often use the flowers she grows for the events she organizes as a party planner. So that left me and my sister, Ally, alone inside for a short amount of time.

I made it to the utility room that adjoined the kitchen, then scooped some of Coda's food out of the tub and into her dog bowl. I'd barely even stood back up before she had already **GOBBLED** the lot.

"You are more like a pig than a dog!" I laughed, ruffling the fur on her head. Coda looked very pleased with herself.

BUUUURP!

"Excuse you!" I said, laughing.

I shuffled over to the fridge,
rubbing my tired eyes, and pulled
out the orange juice. The box felt
light, like there wasn't much left.
I looked from side to side, then
opened the lid and chugged the
remainder of the juice.

"**ARI!**" a voice yelled.

The jump-scare made me spit
the mouthful of juice all over the
kitchen worktop.

"Ally!" I yelled, **ANNOYED**.

My younger sister was standing in the doorway, still in her pyjamas, with her hands on her hips.

"That's *my* juice!" she said, **STOMPING** her foot.

"It's not *your* juice," I argued. "It's the family's juice."

"Well, you just put your gross mouth all over the box. I don't want to drink your slobber," she complained.

"You're in luck," I shot back, "because I've finished it off so you can't drink it anyway."

"You finished my juice?!" she yelled, her face now turning red.

"It's not *your* juice," I repeated, getting louder.

"I like orange juice. You like apple. So that's *my* juice!" she yelled, angry tears filling her eyes.

"You're going to cry about spilt ... juice?!" I yelled back. "You're such a **BABY!**"

"I am not a baby!" Ally **HOLLERED**
like, well, a baby. She took off
a slipper and threw it at me.
I dodged it, and it landed with
a splash into the puddle of juice
on the counter.

"Now my slipper is wet!" she cried.
"It's your fault!"

"You threw it!" I retorted angrily,
swiping my hand across the
counter to **SPLASH** her
with some of the juice.

Her square face turned crimson.
She reached behind her to grab

the closest thing she could find, and hurled the item at me with surprising force.

An egg **SMASHED** on my chest, dripping sticky, gooey yolk down my pyjamas.

"You little rat!" I hollered, leaping past her to get an egg to throw in return.

Ally squealed loudly. She ran away from me, terrified.

"What is going on in here?!" an exasperated voice called.

UH-OH! It was Mum. We hadn't even heard her come in through the back door because of all our yelling.

Mum's arms were full of flower arrangements. She **FROZE** in the doorway as she took in the scene in front of her. Juice all over the worktop. Ally's slipper, wet with sticky juice. Raw egg, dripping down my pyjama shirt and onto the floor. And me, standing in the middle of it all, with an egg in my hand, poised to throw at my sister.

"I can't leave you two alone for five minutes without it turning into chaos!" Mum said angrily, putting the flowers down on the dining table. "Ari, you are meant to be looking after Ally, not attacking her," Mum said.

"IT'S NOT ME!" I yelled back. "She started it. She threw an egg at *me!*"

"I don't want to hear it!" Mum said. "Both of you are in trouble. It's day one of the school holidays and it's already a nightmare. How am I going to get any work done with you two **FIGHTING** like animals all holidays?"

I folded my arms across my chest. This wasnt my fault!

"You'll have to go to holiday care," Mum said, shaking her head.

"Yay!" Ally cheered.

"No, Mum, no!" I protested. "Holiday care is so **LAME,** please don't send me there! Only little kids go and there's never anyone my age. It's for babies!"

"Well, if you act like a baby, you get treated like one," Mum retorted.

"I love holiday care!" Ally sang happily.

"Why is she getting rewarded and I'm getting **PUNISHED?!**" I yelled.

Mum sighed and her expression softened. "You're not being punished with holiday care, Ari," Mum said. "It's fun. You'll go on excursions and play games. It's got to be a lot more interesting than hanging out here with nothing to do."

She did have a point. But there

was no way I was going to hang out there on **MY OWN**.

"Can I at least see if Jez or Zeke want to come?" I asked.

"Yes, of course. In fact, Jez's little brother goes there often, so she might be going anyway," Mum answered. "I'll have a look at the enrolment and choose some days with fun activities. It'll be good."

Hmm. I wasn't so sure.

"In the meantime, you are both on kitchen duty. Clean up the mess you've made, empty the dishwasher and then I want the rubbish taken out," Mum said. "And then you'll be spending the rest of the day spring cleaning your wardrobes."

"**BUT—**" I tried to protest but I reconsidered once I saw Mum's stern expression.

"OK," Ally and I mumbled in unison.

Man, it was only the first day of school holidays and it was already shaping up to be the most **BORING** holiday week ever.

TUESDAY MORNING

BZZZZZZZ!

UGH! Why was my alarm going off during the school holidays?! I was meant to be sleeping in.

Then I **REMEMBERED.** Holiday care day.

Zeke wasn't able to come with me because he'd gone away for the holidays with his family. But at least I'd have my other best friend, Jez. She hadn't planned on going to holiday care, even though her little brother, Max, would be there. But when my mum texted her mum about it, Jez said she'd come along to keep me company. Plus, Tuesday was **EXCURSION DAY**, so at least we weren't stuck at the community centre playing lame little-avatar games.

Today's excursion was a **BOAT RIDE**, followed by lunch on a nearby beach. We would also be given some free time to go swimming, which was cool, I guess.

Mum yelled up the stairs for me and Ally to hurry up, as we had to meet the teachers down by the wharf at 8am sharp. The boat would sail around for a few hours, stopping every now and then to let us swim if the conditions were gentle enough. Then we'd head over to an island for lunch.

I pulled on my clothes and **GRABBED** my rucksack from the floor, thinking about what I'd need for the day. I quickly shoved a beach towel and my sunscreen inside the bag, and then grabbed my water bottle.

Over breakfast, Ally **SCOWLED** at me through her glasses as she chewed her cereal. She was still bitter about me drinking the juice, and even angrier that we had to spend all of yesterday cleaning as punishment for fighting and making a mess.

"Excited to go on the boat?" Mum asked us cheerily, pouring her coffee into a mug.

"Yes!" Ally sang.

"No!" I sang back sarcastically, glaring at my bowl of cereal.

"Ari, cheer up." Mum said. "You'll have Jez there at least. And a day out on a boat? I'm actually quite jealous!"

"A day out with a bunch of **LITTLE KIDS?** It's going to be completely boring!" I said.

The more I thought about the day ahead, the more annoyed I became. I was way too old for holiday care.

"Stop complaining," Mum said. "It's time to go."

TUESDAY MORNING, 8AM

"WHO IS READY TO GO ON AN ADVENTURE?!"

"YAAAAY!" the kids cheered.

I looked at Jez and rolled my

eyes. The teachers at this holiday

care were totally **CRINGEY.**

Ally and Max, Jez's little brother,
stood together looking excited.

"Thanks for coming, Jez," I said to
my friend.

"No sweat," she replied, smiling.
"I know it's a bit **BABYISH**
here, but it's better than sitting
at home doing nothing."

"Is it though?" I replied.

Jez **LAUGHED.** "Think of it this way.

We get a day out at the beach, and our parents think we are being nice older siblings by looking after Ally and Max for the day. So, they're going to be **TOTALLY** nice to us when we get home, which could definitely only work in our favour, right?"

She had a point.

"Well, it's definitely more bearable with you here," I said.

We both looked over to the teacher, who was pretending to be a boat captain. He had a fake captain's hat on and was yelling "All aboard!"

UGH!

Today's excursion group was pretty small, with only ten kids and one teacher. To make it safer, the organizers always limit the number of avatars going on these excursions so the teacher only has a small number of kids to keep an eye on. It was a pretty good thing, because it meant fewer little avatars to annoy us. But it also meant we'd have to stay with Max and Ally the whole time.

We boarded the boat and met the *real* captain, then walked through the cabin to sit in the uncovered area at the back of the boat. As we pulled away from the dock, we waved to our mums, who were still standing near the boathouse.

"Look after Ally!" Mum yelled after me, waving goodbye to us all.

I **ROLLED** my eyes.

Why was it always the job of the eldest avatar in the family to look after the littler ones? Totally **UNFAIR.**

The sun was shining down on us, so I pulled my cap out of my rucksack and placed it on my head. At least it was a sunny day. As the boat picked up speed, a gentle, warm wind whipped across our faces. Jez leaned back, putting her hands behind her head and lifted her feet up onto the seat opposite us.

"See, Ari? This is the **LIFE.**

I reckon today is going to be OK."

I had to admit, it was kinda nice
being out on the water. Maybe
holiday care wasn't so bad after
all. With the warm sun shining
down on my face, my eyes became
heavy. I blinked once. Twice. Then
slowly closed them, drifting off into
a peaceful nap.

TUESDAY — SOME TIME LATER

BANG!

"Everyone, get inside!" a voice hollered.

My eyes snapped open as the boat **JOLTED** sharply. We had stopped abruptly. The boat was wedged against something that was stopping us from moving.

"Inside!" the captain yelled again.

The little avatars **SCREAMED** in fear and ran inside the cabin. Some were crying.

Where's Ally?

"**ALLY!**" I yelled, spotting her picking herself up from the deck of the boat where she'd obviously fallen over.

"Ari, I fell," she whimpered.

I took her hand and led her inside the cabin. As we entered, I overheard the captain speaking in hushed tones to the teacher.

"We've hit a large rock and it's **TORN** the underside of the boat. We're taking on water, fast," he said.

The teacher nodded gravely. He looked from side to side then called me and Jez over.

"Jez, Ari," he said. "You two are my oldest students today, so I'm going to need your **HELP.** You need to do everything the captain tells you, OK?"

Jez and I exchanged worried glances but nodded.

The captain stepped forwards.

"Make sure all the little ones have their **LIFE JACKETS** secure. I'm going to get the lifeboat ready, which we are going to have to board fast. I need you to count the kids as they board. The seas are rough and we can't leave anyone behind."

We nodded again.

In the few minutes we were talking, I could feel the boat taking on more water. We sank deeper into the sea and there was an unmistakable tilt as items from the boat cartwheeled across the deck.

"Avatars!" I yelled. "Everything's going to be OK. You just need to follow me. We need to make a **CHAIN** by holding hands. I'll be at the front, Jez will be at the back," I announced.

The teacher and captain then left Jez and me so they could prepare the lifeboat. By the time we walked with the children to the deck, the adults were already lowering the lifeboat. It splashed into the water, which was now lapping up onto the deck as the boat sank deeper into the cold blue ocean. The waves **CRASHED** against the hull and I worried that the lifeboat wouldn't be able to withstand the strong current and winds.

I counted the kids as they climbed into the lifeboat, one by one. The captain and teacher held the lifeboat steady as each little avatar hopped in.

"Is **EVERYONE** accounted for?" I yelled to Jez over the

crashing waves and buffeting wind.

"Yep, just you, me, Max and Ally
left to get in," she yelled back.

Max clung to Ally's hand, who
was clutching on to Jez.

"OK, now it's your turn," I said to Max and Ally.

"What about you and Jez?" Max **SHOUTED** back tearfully. "I'm not going without my sister."

"Come on, Max," the teacher yelled from the lifeboat. "We are running out of time!"

"Max, I need you to be brave," I said. "We're right behind you."

But he still shook his head.

"It's OK, Max," Jez said soothingly.

'I'll go with you.' Max finally agreed.

But just as Jez and Max stepped up to the edge of the deck, ready to jump into the lifeboat, a **HUGE WAVE** formed,

rising above us in a giant curve.

"TAKE COVER!" I yelled.

Jez, Ally, Max and I ran back inside the main boat's cabin just as the wave hit. It felt like we'd been struck by lightning. The boat **ROCKED** wildly from side to side, and we were thrown about like socks in a dryer.

"Ari!" Jez shrieked, pointing back outside to the deck.

I knew exactly what she was pointing at, as I saw the lifeboat snap away from the boat and get pushed further away from us by the **ROARING** sea. I could see the teacher trying to leap out of the lifeboat to get back to us, but the captain held him back for his own safety.

There was nothing they could do and nothing we could do against the raging seas. We were on our own, and we needed to get off this boat. **FAST.**

TUESDAY—
SECONDS
LATER

As the boat sank deeper, we
knew it would be only a matter
of minutes before it was **SUCKED**
completely under the current. And
we didn't want to be on board
when that happened. Jez and
I looked around with wide eyes,
trying to find something we could
use to keep us afloat.

"The **WORKTOP!**" Jez said,
pointing to the giant bar where

tea and coffee was usually
served.

Jez tried to knock the wooden
counter top off its structure but
it wouldn't budge.

"Stand back," I said, gesturing
for her to pull back the two little
ones. She did, right as I used all
my might to kick the countertop
upwards. The wood splintered off
its base and went **FLYING**
off into the air. We dodged it as
it landed at our feet.

It was a long, thin plank that

I was pretty sure would float. But would it float with four avatars on top of it? We had no time to look for anything else, so Jez and I quickly **GRABBED** the plank and hoped for the best. We told a scared Max and Ally to hold onto us, then we all ran back out onto the deck, which was hardly a deck at all now. Water splashed up over the railing, making it more like a pool. Jez and I gently placed the plank onto the **SWELLING** water. To our relief, it floated!

"Hop on!" I said to Ally and Max.

The two kids gingerly stepped onto the plank.

"Lie on your tummies and hold on," Jez instructed. They did.

"Your turn," I said to Jez.

"Will it hold us all?" she asked, **UNSURE.**

"Only one way to find out," I replied.

Jez lay herself down on the plank. It was hard to get a good grip on the sides with the bulk of the life vest, but she managed to stay on.

Before securing herself with the rope she had grabbed from the cabin, she pulled Ally and Max under her arm to make sure they were protected from the **CRASHING** waves. I could see Ally holding her glasses on her face with one finger.

I slid myself onto the plank to join the others. It bobbed and dipped on the waves under the extra weight, but thankfully it stayed afloat.

"Where are the others?" Jez yelled through the wind.

"I can't see them. I think they've been pulled away from us," I said.

"The captain would have called for help," Jez said. "All we need to do is stay afloat until help arrives."

"That's if we can survive these wild wav—" but I was cut off as a huge wave **CRASHED** onto us.

The impact launched the boat high into the air. Items from the deck came **HURTLING** towards us.

"Protect yourselves!" I yelled, shielding Ally with my body. But

right at that moment, a deck chair
came loose from its buckle.
It spun across the sinking boat
and flew straight towards me.

Then everything went **BLACK.**

TUESDAY —
AROUND
MIDDAY

"Ari?"

Was that Mum's voice, waking
me up?

"Ari, you **NEED** to wake up,"
the voice persisted.

Ugh. It was a dream and now
I have to get up for holiday care.

"Ari, are you OK?"

That's not Mum's voice. That's... that's Jez. Why is Jez in my bedroom?!

I sat up with a start.

"AAAGH!"

"Calm down, you're OK," Jez said soothingly.

I squinted. Everything was bright and my eyes felt gritty. I spat sand out of my mouth and the taste of saltwater sat heavy on my tongue. I looked around and saw we were on land.

And Ally and Max were standing next to Jez. Thank goodness everyone was OK.

"Wha— what happened?" I stammered, looking around.

"You got **HIT** by a chair. Right on the head," Ally said.

I lifted my hand to my hairline where I felt a **STAB** of pain.

"I don't think it's too bad," Jez said. "Bit of a bump, though."

I nodded.

"When the sea calmed down, we floated over to this **ISLAND**," Max said matter-of-factly. "You were still having a nap."

I nodded again.

"So, have you sent for help? Like, have you spoken to anyone on the island?" I said, standing up slowly.

"I - I don't think there *is* anyone,"
Jez replied quietly.

I scanned my surroundings.
The island didn't look too big, from
what I could tell. There was a
large hill - not quite a mountain
- in the middle, obscuring my view
of the other side. The beach was
BARREN and there seemed
to be no sign of avatar life
anywhere.

"But we should be **SAFE** here,"
Jez said. "The captain would have

sent for help. Our rescuers can't
be far off."

"So what now?" Max asked, his
eyes wide.

Jez paused, thinking. "I'm guessing
help will be here soon, but judging
by the sun in the sky, it's probably
just after midday. So if help
doesn't come soon, I think we
should look for **SHELTER**,
just in case..."

She didn't finish her sentence
when she looked at Ally and
Max. I could tell she didn't want

to **SCARE** them. But I knew what she was about to say. *In case we have to stay here overnight.*

"It'll be like a **GAME**," I said brightly, looking at Max and Ally.

Jez looked at me quizzically but quickly caught on.

"Yeah, a game," she added, smiling at the two kids.

"It's like that TV show you like, Ally," I said. "The one where they have to **SURVIVE** on the desert island."

Ally looked doubtful.

"Yeah. We just have to play survival here for a bit, and then we'll be rescued," Jez encouraged.

"I can help!" Max said **EAGERLY.** He was a bit younger than Ally and easier to convince.

Ally shrugged.

"First, we need to collect materials to make a **HOUSE** for us here. Like a den!" Jez said. "But we're going to stick together while we search. No separating."

It was a good plan.

"Ally and Max, can you find palm fronds for the roof?" I asked. I **JOGGED** up the sand to where the beach ended and the plants started. I picked up a long palm frond off the ground. "Like these!"

"I can do that!" Max said. "I'm very **STRONG!**"

"Yeah, you are, Max," Jez smiled. "You can find the palm fronds from this area," she said, pointing to the treeline, "and pile them up over here where we'll set up a shelter."

Max and Ally started to drag
palm fronds into a pile.

"And grab anything else you find
too – shells, coconuts – anything!"
I added.

"Ari, we'll also need **BAMBOO**.
The structure needs to be strong
enough to keep us dry during any
wild weather," Jez said.

I nodded. The weather looked OK
at the moment. But neither of us
had any idea how long we would
be here. Hours? Days? *Weeks?*
I **SWALLOWED** hard.

"Look what I found!" Max declared, holding up a couple of old tin cans.

"Ew, leave that **RUBBISH** alone!" Ally said.

"No, that's perfect!" said Jez. "We need things to boil our water in. Which brings me to the next thing we need to do. We need **FIRE.**"

"How do you start a fire without matches?" Ally asked, who was wiping sea salt from her glasses.

I looked at Jez. She was thinking the same thing I was.

"Ally," Jez said, "I'm going to need to borrow your glasses."

"Why?" Ally said, stepping back to protect her glasses. Ally's vision isn't the best so she's always been careful to keep her glasses with her at all times.

"The **GLASS** can help us start a fire," Jez said.

I nodded at Ally encouragingly, who then reluctantly handed over her precious glasses.

We picked out a space for our

shelter, then cleared the area. Jez arranged the light husks from the palms into a little ball, then dug a shallow hole in the sand and placed the kindling inside.

"I learned this in Scouts," she said. "We need things that will **BURN** fast to start the fire. Then, we build sturdier sticks around it to keep the flame going."

Jez looked up at the sun and held Ally's glasses close to the husks. It took her some time, but after moving them around to get the perfect angle, she finally got the sun's rays to shine through the glass and into a little pinpoint on the husks. A tiny thread of **SMOKE** spiralled out from the kindling.

"You're doing it!" Max yelled, proud of his big sister.

"Not quite yet," Jez whispered. She handed back Ally's glasses, then breathed lightly onto the smoke.

"Don't **BLOW** it out!" Ally said, alarmed.

"She's not," I said, remembering a particular science class. "Fire needs oxygen to burn. So she's giving it oxygen."

The smoke sparked, and with a few more light breaths, shone

brighter until it **BURST** into a single flame. Jez quickly began to pack bigger sticks around the fire, hoping they would catch. The small **FLAMES** slowly licked the sticks, and finally caught. Now with a larger fire to work with, Jez slowly built heavier sticks around the flame in a pyramid, adding more and more larger sticks as the flames grew higher.

"**EPIC!**" I yelled, as Jez stood up to admire her handiwork.

"Now we can keep warm and boil water to drink," she said, smiling.

Suddenly, a strange **RUMBLING** sound came through the air. Was it a plane? Were we saved already?

GRRRRRRRRRRRR.

"Ari," Jez whispered. "It's coming from the top of the hill."

TUESDAY — AFTERNOON

Jez and I spent the rest of the afternoon distracting Max and Ally from the strange rumbling sound that **ECHOED** out from the top of the hill. It wasn't too hard to do, because we kept them very **BUSY.** After only a few hours, we had built a small shelter, collected some coconuts and boiled water on our new fire. Ally had even decorated the shelter with some flowers to make it 'more pretty and homely'.

After we had our shelter and clean water, Max and Jez then spent some time spelling out SOS in **MASSIVE** writing in the sand, in case someone flew over the island in a plane looking for us. Meanwhile, I spent that time standing on the shore, examining the horizon for any sign of a ship.

But there was nothing.

I didn't want to take my eyes off the vast ocean, in case I missed our only chance of rescue, but my stomach **RUMBLED** and I couldn't ignore the pull of food.

"Ally," I said to my sister, who was now sitting next to me on the shoreline. "Wanna help me look for something to **EAT?**"

She looked away from the horizon and nodded eagerly. She was probably just as hungry as I was.

Thankfully, our island seemed pretty plentiful when it came to fruits. We'd gathered coconuts and plantains, which were a bit like bananas. We also found pawpaw, which were ripe and sweet inside. We cut the fruit up for dinner and ate it **HUNGRILY.**

TUESDAY — EVENING

As the sun began to dip below the skyline, **NERVOUS** butterflies fluttered around in my stomach. I didn't like the thought of having to sleep out in the wilderness overnight. But then we looked out to the horizon, and I instantly felt better. The sky had turned a blend of pink and orange with swirls of light purple.

It was **BREATHTAKING.** And it somehow calmed me.

Jez stoked the fire so the flames
rose higher and we huddled
together around the warmth.
But Max and Ally started to
look **WORRIED** as the sky became
darker and night arrived.

"Hey, I know," I said. "Let's do some
STAR GAZING. Look up
there!" I said, pointing to the sky.
"Can you see how the stars make
the shape of a dragon?" I pointed
my finger to a group of stars
directly above us and joined them
together with an invisible line.

"Oh, yeah!" said Max, brightening.

"I can see a **LOLLYPOP!**"
Ally said, pointing to another
cluster of stars to our right.

Max let out a big **YAWN.**

"I think it's time to get you two
avatars to bed," Jez said, looking
at our sleepy siblings.

Max and Ally lay down on the
leaf beds we had created earlier
that day. Then we tucked them in
with big **PALM FRONDS** to
keep the night air off them.

"Ari?" Ally said sleepily. "Do you

think we'll be rescued tomorrow?"

"I'm sure we will," I said with a **WAVER** in my voice. "Just go to sleep now."

"Ari?" she said again.

"Ally, I said go to sleep," I said, a little irritated.

"I know. I just wanted to say thanks. For looking after us."

My cheeks **FLUSHED** pink and my eyes felt a prickle in them.
"Oh. That's cool," I said.

Then Ally and Max drifted off to sleep, snoring softly.

Jez and I sat by the fire, keeping warm and talking about what we would do if we actually weren't **RESCUED** tomorrow.

"We can't live off fruit," I said.
"Our stomachs will not appreciate
that for long. We'll need to fish or
find a vegetable."

Jez nodded under the moonlight.

GRRRRRRRRRRRRRRRRRRR!

The low rumble from the hill
grew louder.

"Ari, I don't know what that sound
is, but it worries me," Jez said, and
I had to agree. "We need a backup
plan. A safety plan to escape
whatever that is, if we need to."

I knew Jez was right. It may have
been the rumble of a volcano —
or worse, a creature — whatever
it was, I didn't want to be caught
with no way off this island.

WEDNESDAY — EARLY MORNING

"Wake up, sleepy heads! We made you **BREAKFAST!**" a little voice chirped.

I slowly opened my eyes to see Ally and Max standing there with a bunch of fruit laid out on a palm leaf.

"Oh, **WOW!** Thanks, guys," Jez said, sitting up slowly and rubbing the sleep from her eyes.

"I think the **MOUNTAIN** is hungry too," Max said in between bites of mango. "It's had a grumbly tummy all morning!"

Jez and I looked at each other with wide eyes. The rumbling had evolved into a low grade **HUM.** It was deeper and more droning than last night's growl. Jez and I needed to find another distraction for the two little avatars.

"OK," Jez said, suddenly standing up. "We're going to play something different today. We're going to ... uhh ... build a **BOAT!**"

"To hunt for treasure?" Max asked with wide eyes.

"Sure," I said, jumping in on Jez's plan. "We're going to make a cool boat to sail the seven seas!"

"**YAY!**" Max and Ally chorused.

"What we need to do first is find more bamboo," Jez said, tapping one of the hollow bamboo pipes that held up our make-shift shelter. "They are nice and light so they'll float. But we'll need a **LOT.** And a lot of palm leaf husks to use as twine."

"Aye, aye, Captain!" Max saluted.

"Remember to stay close," I reminded them. Man, I was really starting to sound like Mum.

We wandered around, collecting the bamboo pipes and creating a pile near our shelter. Jez tended the fire and kept boiling and cooling water to keep us all hydrated. As the pile of bamboo got bigger, I began to line the pieces up and tie them together using **KNOTS** that I'd learned from Zeke's dad. He's in the army, so the knots he taught me were

strong and should last. I tested
the raft every now and then,
checking it was sturdy. So far,
so good.

I looked above at the sun. It was
still arcing up to the centre of the
sky, so we had plenty of time to
finish our raft in daylight. But as
the low **BUZZING** noise continued
to hum, I wondered if we'd need to
use the raft sooner than expected.

WEDNESDAY — AN HOUR LATER

"Done!" I yelled triumphantly.

The raft was **COMPLETE.**

Each bamboo log was bound together tightly, and the raft was big enough to fit all four of us. I had taken it down to one of the deep, still-water rock pools by the shore and was satisfied to see it floated, even while I was sitting on it. I was confident we could use it if we needed to **ESCAPE** the island fast. I still wasn't sure where we'd be safest — on land with whatever was grumbling and buzzing, or at sea with the wind and the waves.

"**ARI! ARI!**" I heard Jez yelling from our camp.

I pulled the raft out of the rock
pool and back onto the sand.
Then I jogged up the beach to
see what was happening.

"Where did you see her last?" Jez
said to Max urgently.

"What's going on?" I asked.

"Ally is **MISSING**," Jez said.

"Missing?! We said stay together!
Max, what happened?" I said.

Max looked up at me with wide
eyes. "I told her not to go, but she

wouldn't listen," he said, sniffing. "She saw a deer and she chased it up the hill. She thought it might be able to help us."

FACEPALM!

The buzzing grew **LOUDER.**

"I have to go find her," I said. "You two wait here."

"No way," said Jez. "I'm not having you disappear, too. Max and I are coming. We need to stick together."

I looked at Jez, and then looked

up the large hill. There was no
time to argue.

"Come on," I said **URGENTLY**,
walking off into the dense scrub
in search of my little sister.

WEDNESDAY—
A BIT LATER

"My legs are sore," Max whined.

I knew we shouldn't have all gone looking for Ally.

"Max, are you **SURE** she went this way?" I asked again for the fifth time.

He nodded but looked unsure. We had been **BASHING** through the dense scrub, calling Ally's name for half an hour. I had a big thick stick in my hand and was using it to clear a path for us to travel through. But as we climbed the steep hill, the rumbling buzz grew louder and louder.

"What's that noise?" Max asked. The noise was too loud to ignore.

"I'm sure it's nothing," Jez said, dismissing the question.

"AAAAGH!"

Max screamed as a **HUGE WASP** came hurtling towards him. It was bigger than any wasp

I'd ever seen — as big as my head! I could see its sharp stinger protruding from the back of it as it flew **ANGRILY** around Max.

"Duck for **COVER!**" Jez yelled, throwing a palm leaf at Max to protect himself.

But the wasp continued to swoop around him. Until it turned and saw me and Jez and decided to change its attack plan.

It flew towards Jez, the sharp point of it's stinger **GLISTENING** in the afternoon sun. As it prepared to sting her, I quickly leaped out in front of her and **SWIPED** at it with my large stick. My makeshift weapon connected with the wasp's head, sending it **HURTLING** through the air before it slammed into a tree and fell to the ground.

"That was *huge*," Jez breathed.
"I really hope we don't run into
any more of those!"

"Um, Jez?" Max said in a shaky
voice, looking through some shrubs
just ahead of us.

"What is it?" Jez said, walking up
to join him.

"There," Max said, pointing. Jez's
mouth fell wide open in **SHOCK.**

"Ari," she said shakily. "You need
to see this."

WEDNESDAY — EVEN LATER

I peered through the scrub to see that we'd reached the top of the mountain. But it was in that moment that I also realized that this little mountain — this 'hill' we had been climbing the whole time — was no hill at all. There was a huge **OPENING** at the peak, much like a volcano's crater. But this was no volcano.

Wasps in various sizes **HOVERED** around the opening. Some were as big as the one that just attacked Max, which we'd thought was huge. Turns out they were nothing compared to the rest. Some wasps were as big as an avatar, and the largest ones were as big as a **HORSE.**

"Ari, I don't think this is a hill,"
Jez whispered.

I shook my head. "You're right Jez.
This is ... a nest. A **WASP'S
NEST.**"

I swallowed hard as the realization
took over me. Our island wasn't
really an island. It was a giant
wasp's nest that lived in the
middle of the ocean. The constant
buzz and rumbling we'd heard
while here had been the ominous
hum of **ANGRY** wasps the
whole time. And it didn't sound like
they were happy to have visitors.

We sank to the floor and
CRAWLED on our bellies to get
a closer look at the opening of
the nest. We had to be careful to
stay hidden. But we also had to
find Ally.

Then we heard it.

"HEEEEELP!"

"That's Ally!" I whispered urgently.

The sound was coming from
INSIDE the nest.

"Jez and Max, I want you to stay

here. There's no point in all of us getting trapped. I'm going to go inside the nest and see if I can find my sister."

I could tell Jez wanted to protest, but she nodded **GLUMLY** instead. There was no way she could look after Max and help me to save Ally, and she knew it. Jez pulled her little brother in close as he trembled by her side.

I pulled a large palm leaf over my body and commando crawled beneath the hovering wasps to the rim of the nest. The buzzing grew angry, as if the creatures sensed an **INTRUDER** in their midst.

I peered over the edge of the opening and immediately saw Ally. She was **IMPRISONED** in a makeshift cage that the wasps had created in the nest's wall. She looked **TERRIFIED.**

Guarding the cage wall were some of the smaller wasps – and by smaller, I mean they were still as big as me! I needed to create a **DIVERSION** to get the guard wasps to leave their post.

I looked around wildly, trying to find something to distract them. Then I saw a large **BOULDER**, precariously poised on the side of the nest. It could be exactly what I needed.

Using the leaf for cover, I commando crawled around the rim of the nest until I reached the

boulder. I tried to **PUSH** it with
my arms while under the leaf.
It shifted a millimetre, but wasn't
moving more than that.

I saw a large stick on the ground.
A thought jumped into my mind – I
could use the stick as a lever,
but that would mean breaking my
cover. Would I have time to hoist
the boulder off the edge of the
nest, or would the wasps get to
me first?

I heard Ally calling for help from
inside the nest and I knew I only
had one choice.

WEDNESDAY — A FEW MINUTES LATER

In one swift motion, I **JUMPED** out from under the leaf and grabbed the heavy stick. I glanced behind me and saw some of the wasps look in my direction. Suddenly, there was a **DEAFENING** buzz as the wasps headed towards me.

I dragged the stick — which was more like a log — over to the nest edge and wedged it under the boulder. Once it was firmly in place, I pushed down on it, hoping to lift the boulder up, but the stick wouldn't move.

The hum of angry wasps grew **LOUDER.** They would reach me soon — I had to hurry.

I thought of Zeke and his epic **PARKOUR** skills. I jumped into the air and landed hard on the top of the stick, pushing my body downwards. The stick sank under the pressure of my weight and dislodged the boulder!

It tipped then rolled, **CRASHING** loudly down the hill. I pulled myself back under the leaf while the wasps zoomed above me, **CHASING** the boulder as it hurtled towards the beach.

Slowly, the angry buzz of the swarm softened. I cautiously lifted my head and looked around.

The guard wasps were gone and the buzzing sounded far off down the hill. I threw the leaf off my body and ran over to the edge of the nest.

"ALLY!" I yelled.

Ally looked up at me with a tear stained face. "Ari! SAVE ME!"

I carefully climbed down into the nest and landed on one of the platforms that jutted out from the nest's wall.

"Stand back, Ally," I warned.

I took a run up and did a flying parkour kick into the door of the cage. It **SHATTERED** under the impact of my foot and Ally came running out, throwing her arms around me.

"I'm so sorry," she wept.

"It's OK, Ally. We just need to get

out of here," I said. "The swarm will be back soon."

I instructed Ally to climb onto my back. It was going to be the easiest way to get her out of there. Then I began to climb the ragged nest walls, which was much **HARDER** with my sister clinging to my back. But I climbed on, powered by my own desperation.

We finally reached the top and I **COLLAPSED** with exhaustion. Jez and Max then came running out of hiding and embraced Ally.

"We need to get out of here,"
Jez said.

Suddenly, a low rumbling sounded
from deep within the nest.
The walls of the nest **VIBRATED**
with the angry buzz and Jez and
I looked at each other in fear.
And then, out from the top of the
nest, rose a gigantic wasp the
size of a car.

"I think we've just met the
QUEEN," I gulped.

WEDNESDAY— EVEN LATER

The queen wasp rose into the air, wings batting like an eagle. Her **STINGER** was longer than a baseball bat, with a sharp end that glistened in the sunlight.

She rose high above the nest and let out a long, loud **BUZZ.**

Suddenly, the collective buzz from the swarm rose up from its position down the hill.

She was calling her soldiers.

"**RUN!**" I screamed, grabbing Ally's hand.

But before we could leave down the hill, we saw movement through a clearing in the trees. The swarm came into view. They looked furious and had their stingers pointed in our direction.

"We're going to get **STUNG** to death!" Max cried.

We looked around wildly for an escape. It was going to be hard to outrun them, and there was a high chance we'd get stung on the way down if we ran through the swarm. I'd been stung by a small wasp once before, and boy was it painful. Being stung by one of these big wasps would mean certain **DEATH.** I looked around for a way to escape.

"THERE!" I yelled, pointing to a large, hollow log.

"We can't **HIDE**," Jez said. "They'll just guard us until we come out!"

"I'm not planning on hiding," I said. "The log is for protection, yes, but we're not staying here!"

We all ran over to the log.

"Ally, remember that time at the fair when we rode inside the **ORBS?**" I said as I tried to hurry the others inside the log.

"You mean the big, inflatable balls we used to **ROLL DOWN** the hill?" she asked.

I nodded. "Well, this is just like that. Get in!"

Jez looked at me doubtfully, and I could tell what she was thinking, *I sure hope this works.*

Once Max, Ally and Jez were

inside, I instructed them to brace themselves on anything they could.

The **BUZZING** continued, getting louder. A small wasp caught up with me, but I was able to use my stick to bat it away before it could sting me.

I then sat down behind the log, and, using all the power of my legs, **PUSHED** hard against it. It shifted and began to tip. I bolted around the side and jumped in through the opening to join the others, just as the log picked up momentum.

"Here we go!" I yelled, pushing my weight forwards to speed up the rolling log.

The log **TUMBLED** down the hill, rolling round and round. We all pushed our hands and legs against the walls of the log to prevent us from being scrambled – I didn't feel like becoming an avatar milkshake!

As the log rolled down the hill at rapid speed, I could still hear the buzzing of the **WASPS** following close behind as they raced to keep up with us.

WHOOOOOOAAAAAAAAAA!

THUD!

The log finally hit the bottom
of the hill, stopped by the sand
on the beach. We crawled out,
completely dizzy, and fell over
onto the sand.

"We have to keep going" I yelled,
trying to stand up. I fell to the
ground with dizziness.

BUZZZZZZZZZ!

Instructing the others to follow me,

we **CRAWLED** on our hands and knees down the beach while we regained our balance.

As soon as we reached my raft, Jez and I dragged it over to the small waves that lapped gently against the shore.

"Get on!" I instructed the little ones.

Max and Ally jumped on while Jez and I continued to **PUSH** the raft further into the water.

Once we were out far enough, Jez and I joined the smaller avatars on the raft. We picked up the paddles that I'd made out of long sticks and husks and began to paddle as hard as we could.

BUZZZZZZZZZ!

Some of the wasps had followed us out over the water, so we used our paddles to bat them away.

"We just have to get far away enough that they won't think we're a **THREAT** anymore. They should leave us alone," Jez said.

I really hoped she was right.

We paddled hard, the waves pummelling us as we went.

Finally, we made it past the breaking waves and out to the calmer waters beyond. Thankfully, Jez was right about the wasps. The ones that had followed us over the water started to slow their pursuit, turning around to fly back to the safety of land. Eventually, the buzzing of the wasps subsided.

We **COLLAPSED** onto the raft in utter exhaustion.

WEDNESDAY—
1 HOUR LATER

None of us spoke or moved.
Even though an hour had passed,
we were still exhausted from
escaping the wasp nest. But now,
we faced a completely **NEW
PROBLEM.** We were floating
out at sea with no food or water,
no life vests and no way home.

Suddenly, a low **DRONING** caused
me to jump in fear.

I bolted upright. "They're back?!"

I scanned the horizon and my heart dropped when I saw the queen wasp **FLYING** towards us, her huge wings vibrating loudly in the distance.

"TAKE COVER! I cried.

But it wasn't the queen wasp at all.

It was a **HELICOPTER!**

"We're being rescued!" Max yelled.

We waved our arms in the air and yelled at the top of our lungs.

The helicopter flew closer and **HOVERED** just above us. A ladder then dropped down and a rescue soldier in a harness descended.

"Boy, am I glad to see you four," he said, laughing with relief.

"Not as happy as we are to see *you!*" Jez replied.

The rescue soldier hooked Max and Ally on to his harness and was **PULLED** back up into the helicopter. Then he returned to grab me and Jez.

Once we were all safely seated in the chopper, I let out a huge sigh of relief. We were **SAVED!**

Ally sat next to me and leaned her head on my shoulder. For half a second, I thought about pushing her off me – I mean, who wants their little sister leaning on them?! But then I saw her look up at me and she **SMILED.**

"Thanks for saving me, Ari," she whispered.

I put my arm around her and let her rest against my body. Within a few minutes of flying she was fast asleep.

SATURDAY MORNING

It had been a few days since our big island adventure. As soon as we made it back to the mainland, we were taken to the hospital to be checked out. Then, once we were given the all-clear, we were interviewed for the **NEWS!**

We also found out that all the other avatars from the holiday care had made it back safely within an hour of being separated from us.

Ally and I sat at the breakfast table, eating our waffles.
Dad was at work down at the docks and Mum was hurrying around preparing a party event.

"I have to run to the florist and pick up some flower arrangements," she said, grabbing her bag. "Ally, you'd better come with me so you two don't **FIGHT** while I'm out."

"It's OK, Mum," I said. "I think Ally and I will be fine here, right, Al?"

Ally looked at me and broke into a huge smile.

"We sure will!" she grinned.

"We could play a **COMPUTER GAME** together," I suggested. "That new horse racing game you've had your eyes on came out while we were gone. Wanna give it a go?"

Ally's eyes went wide, slightly shocked at my offer, but she couldn't hide her excitement.

"YEAH!"

Mum also seemed a little shocked, but smiled anyway. "OK, well, I'll only be five minutes. Are you sure you two will be fine while I'm gone?"

We both nodded.

"Absolutely," I said. "I've got you, Ally."

Because she knew I did, no matter how many eggs we threw at one another.

ALSO AVAILABLE:

AND EVEN MORE
ROBLOX
ADVENTURES
COMING SOON!

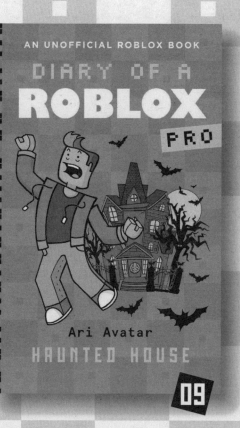